A Spark in the Darkness

Kate Young

First published 2022 by The Hedgehog Poetry Press

Published in the UK by
The Hedgehog Poetry Press
5, Coppack House
Churchill Avenue
Clevedon
BS21 6QW

www.hedgehogpress.co.uk

ISBN: 978-1-913499-16-7

Copyright © Kate Young 2022

The right of Kate Young to be identified as the author of this work has been asserted in accordance with the Copyright, Designs and Patents Act 1988.

All rights reserved. No part of this publication may be reproduced, stored in or introduced into a retrieval system, or transmitted in any form, or by any means (electronic, mechanical, photocopying, recording or otherwise) without prior written permissions of the publisher. Any person who does any unauthorised act in relation to this publication may be liable for criminal prosecution and civil claims for damages,

9 8 7 6 5 4 3 2 1

A CIP Catalogue record for this book is available from the British Library.

*For Trish, who always believed in my poetry
and would have been so very proud.*

Contents

A Breath of Beauty 6
#birdstakeovertheworld 8
The Passing of Hugs 9
No Ordinary Apothecary 10
The Problem with Armchairs 12
Waiting to be Astonished 13
Firefly in the Doorway 14
A suitcase full of parts 15
The Unpeel of Ruin 16
Stealer of Darkness 18
The Girl Beyond the Wheelchair 19
Ring of Rye Harbour 20
Words 21

Acknowledgements 23
About Kate Young 24

A BREATH OF BEAUTY

A flirtation of clouds collides,
releases a silent collusion
of vapour. It seeps into lungs
and we fear we may drown.

Lockdown brings meditation,
limbs splayed in hazy warmth
soft-lined as feline fur
absorbing Dawn's gift.

Slowly, I unwrap it,
slide Sellotape from eyes
to unfold a new world.
It drops in my lap like a gem.

I roll facets between fingers,
catch the nuance of light,
the way sunrise unrolls its smile.
How did I miss first blush of day?

I was never a moment-seeker,
thoughts stumbling ahead of feet,
a shadow-tracker counting steps
but today I lift, Time stalled.

I catch the shift of bud to bloom,
the way creamy clusters
of bawled fists unfurl,
and I open myself to receive:

a syncopation of birdsong
strung across the sky,

a tickle of childish laughter
slipping under fences,

a rustle of bugs in roots
hedged in thistle and stump,

a sweep of bruised aubretia
spread over walls,

a steal of magpies in copper crown
lording over its bounty.

My lungs expand, drink in
a breath of beauty, exhale.

#BIRDSTAKEOVERTHEWORLD

Drunk on fresh-laundered air
a spillage of starlings alight,
as if thrown from Royal Oak
for cheeky lunchtime binging,

a flight of dotted patternation
fills a vacant sky,
looping in victory roll,
vapour trails extinct,

blackbird perched as lookout
stalks a street, wings-a-quiver,
the rattle of an empty bus
ghosting through hollow towns,

raucous song descends,
joins illicit gatherings,
sparrows stagger over park
all totter and twig-legs

cocked heads, needle-eyes
poking fun at Twitter feed,
a growing murmuration-
#birdstakeovertheworld.

THE PASSING OF HUGS

Metallic shelves lie barren, glisten,
beg with open arms to be fed,

pints, like punters, waiting to be pulled
lie vacant in a contactless void,

cutlery winks from once full bars
a silent celebration of parties past,

people scurry two metres apart,
a grey approximation of safety,

they talk with eyes, sound in mask,
footfall and mouths swallowed in fear,

cocoons appear, we wrap the unseen,
discard all touch like tissue, soiled,

empty playgrounds grieve their loss,
the scraped knees, laughter, spats,

nets lie empty, balls un-kicked,
bats and sticks craving warmth,

fingers dance across internet sites,
spread contagion with pulsing alarm,

a huddle of mourners gathers, defiant,
a howl escapes, hugs are exchanged.

NO ORDINARY APOTHECARY

I am no ordinary apothecary,
you will not ingest my vials
chemically
pharmaceutically
but naturally,
a spiritual remedy
from inside out
not outside in.

From my hand- sculpted box
I will source for you

reflective shards
of broken mirror
so you can see all angles,

a splinter of wood
to dig out prescription
printed on paper, ailing,

a glass of sand
to buy you time
before it runs away,

a bottled shell
so you can hear
an echoed cry for help,

a gasp of coral
to give you underwater breath
when you are drowning,

a cork bobbing
to keep you afloat
when champagne bubbles pop,

a flight of feathers
to raise your spirit,
wings to soar, healed.

THE PROBLEM WITH ARMCHAIRS

How stiff you sit
in the old armchair,
devoid of arms
to hold, comfort,
its harsh edges
defining your pain.

"It is time", you sigh,
to let your fingers
loosen their grip,
slip from the world
seamlessly, gifting
strands of memory.

"It is time", I reply,
to lift the sash
just a crack
let a slither of spring
squeeze in,
scent heady with bluebells.

"Look!", you smile,
for on the sill sits
a familiar sentinel,
vibrato rattling the air,
voice as sleek
as petrol blue feathers
quivering, sensing
opportunity for flight.

"Gently", I exhale, as you
peel away the layers of day,
breathe in her colours,
her sparkly robe
clothed in hope
and rise with the call.

WAITING TO BE ASTONISHED

As a child I collected atoms of possibility,
a fluid, golden string of beads
some full of hope, others of fear.

My Granny gathered pebbles from beaches,
urged me to transfer fear to stone
safely stored in glass stoppered bottles

as if containment could make dread disappear,
the underside of gritty sand rubbed smooth,
erasing sharp chins of chance from rock.

She was full of superstition and liquor,
my Granny, preferred to stash omens
swirling like amber grain in her brain.

But decanter slowly shifted, floor tilted
the bottle toppled from table edge
released a scatter of thoughts with a glug.

Fears spilt in an arc, shuffled
at random as cards from the Tarot,
re-arranged the patterns of fate.

Myself, I prefer to think of hope,
its round vowels an open mouth
waiting to be astonished.

FIREFLY IN THE DOORWAY

You entered, a small fireball of fury
limbs crumpled beneath supple skin,
fists and vocals demanding freedom.

Destined to shine you cut a path
through city cubes, manoeuvred curves
like a diamond, your energy priceless.

I think of you as an iridescent moon
softly pulling the blue from the mournful,
your reflection skating on glass kerbs.

You illuminate the sky with speckled hope,
the flicker-flack of firefly, your aura
confident as a spark in the darkness

despair unwrapped from the jumbled hitch
and fold of this creased-up world,
dazzling in the shade of a doorway.

A SUITCASE FULL OF PARTS.

So young, so full of questions
my gem of a treasure box child,
always turning stones over
feeling their rub,
his toddler eyes wide with delight.

I follow his gaze to a zircon sky
where vapour trails merge
criss-crossing,
soft edged pearls, the tears of the gods
falling like milk teeth.

"God's suitcase must be huge", he ponders
arms outstretched to indicate width,
an albatross hovering over truth,
"for all the spare parts" he enunciates clearly
"how else does he put people together?"

I laugh at the thought,
God's very own click-and-collect bone store!
My mind absorbs his drops of innocence
but he has moved on
creating stories from pearly-swirl clouds.

THE UNPEEL OF RUIN

A moon paddles in shallows.
I hardly recognise myself,
the shrivelled skin of lemon.
So begins the unpeel of ruin.

Tide has lost her balance.
She teeters on the crest
of instability, recovers,
restores the hand of gravity.

I drag reflection from wetlands,
reverse the sapphire glacier
its scarp-edged pick of spoil
and lift it clear of fjord-flood.

I am spell-bound, mesmerised
as slick-black oceans gasp,
refreshed by the re-ebb
and flow of coastal surf,

cool as balm on bleached reef
where pinkened lungs re-inflate,
mottled shells of flatbacks flip
right-side-up, un-extinct.

A glut of plastic-nurdles
regurgitate from gill and gut.
Oil and gas back-suck in well
a quash of drill untwists,

floods recede, droughts expire
urban sprawl of timber, brick,
dismantle slowly slab-on-slab,
a graveyard of machinery.

Axe retracts from ancient bark,
canopies re-grow their spread,
light flickers, life in vine
dances to the thrum of rain.

A moon basks in streams.
My crescent- lips smile back
at dunes, headland, knoll, bay
and Earth holds her breath.

STEALER OF DARKNESS

I Stand on the edge of beauty.
To the East, Uluru clothed in night-shadow
a whisper of Outback breath fresh on skin.

I cut artificial light from screen.
My stealer of darkness lies, naked in shame
diminished by the spectacular.

I tilt, neck at 45 to gaze at upturned cave.
It descends, sprinkles its cosmic dust,
starburst blaze from tip of wand

and I am drawn toward dome,
lost in its spirals, its violet freckles
random patterns of pinwheel-spin.

Sirius conjures Ursa Major, the hunt,
her constellation pinned in time
her bears weightless in a veiled sky.

Orion is wearing her indigo smile, it is
splattered across the sheer expanse of space,
leaving the shape of me   floating

THE GIRL BEYOND THE WHEELCHAIR

Today I caught a mermaid,
a real one curved
like the shape of breath,
not flattened
by the weight of page.

She was beautiful,
an oyster shell
opening herself to sun
yet wrapped
in her own company

while those around
unfolded their limbs
and flung them
across seas of pebbles
leached of colour.

A seal, draped on stone,
she lowered herself
seat to salt
buoyant in ocean tide
and dived beneath the surface

leaving her silken tail
to drop, to drip
its string of tiny pearls
caught in spokes
of wheels on chair.

I loosened the strands
of trapped sarong
and placed it on her seat.
Today I caught a mermaid,
she was living, felt free.

RING OF RYE HARBOUR

It is sullen today, the River Rother,
a refugee running from its source
looking for openings, an ocean maybe
as welcoming as Camber,
her golden arms outstretched
inviting the sea like a child to breast,
nurturing, comforting.

In the distance pockets of colour
are scattered like packets of skittles,
the polka dots of bikini tops
and brashly coloured beach hut hats
invading a landscape clothed for subtlety.

The day feels grey, rasping as a gull's gasp
but summer settles mid-throne and gloats.
Contentment seeps through fair-weather cloud,
opals shining on the ring of Rye Harbour.
There is hardly a whisper on the water
yet the wind whips my hair and gulping air
I turn towards triangular steel arms,
a colony of silent beasts graceful in rotation
now native to this beautifully preserved reserve.

There is a quiet confidence here,
the way the teasels tempt attraction.
Puce sweet peas invade hush of grass,
they remind me of sparkling jewels cut
on a plain gold band, a fusing of old and new.

WORDS

Today you gifted me a key,
a silver key, slim as a secret.
I slipped it neatly into the link
and released the catch with caution.

Inside lay an ocean of paper,
wave after wave of wordless pages
bobbing, billowing expectant,
like streaming sails.

Slowly, I raised the pen,
an old friend, a familiar hand.
It settled, heavy in my palm
filling the cracks instinctively.

At first, the lines leaden with disuse
scratched and scraped across the verse,
words stumbled over similes
or drifted away on the tide

but the gift is alive-
it bubbles and foams unexpectedly,
spews its fresh thoughts onto shores
like a shoal of prose.

ACKNOWLEDGEMENTS

I would like to thank my poet friends in Mid Kent Stanza for their continued encouragement and support over the last few years. Also, members of the Open University Poets whose Zoom sessions have been invaluable and Lorette at *The Ekphrastic Review* who has been an influence on my writing journey. My thanks go to Mark Davidson at Hedgehog Press for his faith in my work and for giving me the opportunity to publish this pamphlet.

Some poems in this pamphlet first appeared in:
Poetry on the Lake, Beyond the Storm, The Ekphrastic Review, Ninemuses and *Words for the Wild*

ABOUT KATE YOUNG

Kate Young grew up in Norwich where she completed her teaching degree. She moved to Kent in 1978 to start a long teaching career and still enjoys the odd day working in KS1. She lives with her husband, her grown-up children having 'flown the nest'! She has been passionate about poetry and literature since childhood.

Her work has appeared in *Ninemuses, The Ekphrastic Review, Words for the Wild, Poetry on the Lake, Sea Changes, The Poet, The Alchemy Spoon, Dreich, Fly on the Wall Press, Poetry Scotland, City, Town & Village, Boundaries & Borders* and *New Ways of Looking at Rye Harbour*.

She has also been published in the anthologies *Places of Poetry* and *Beyond the Storm*. Some of her poems appeared in *Liberté, égalité, fraternité*, published by Hedgehog Press.

She was placed 3rd in the Vernal Equinox Competition in 2021, won the Tiny Things competition from Stirling Makar and was commended in the 2022 Indigo Poetry Prize.

Find her on Twitter @Kateyoung12poet.

www.ingramcontent.com/pod-product-compliance
Lightning Source LLC
Chambersburg PA
CBHW021455080526
44588CB00009B/864